GENERAL ORDERS,
No. 1.

WAR DEPARTMENT,
ADJUTANT GENERAL'S OFFICE,
Washington, January, 1863.

The following Proclamation by the President, for the
information and government of the Army and the

BY THE PRESIDENT OF THE UNITED STATES OF AMERICA.

A PROCLAMATION.

WHEREAS, on the twenty-second day of September, in the year of
our Lord one thousand eight hundred and sixty-two, a Proclamation

A Primary Source History of

THE U.S. CIVIL WAR

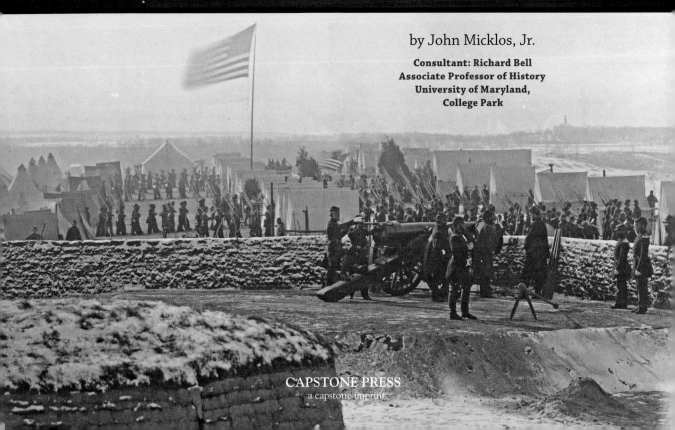

by John Micklos, Jr.

Consultant: Richard Bell
Associate Professor of History
University of Maryland,
College Park

CAPSTONE PRESS
a capstone imprint

Fact Finders Books are published by Capstone Press,
1710 Roe Crest Drive, North Mankato, Minnesota 56003
www.mycapstone.com

Copyright © 2016 by Capstone Press, a Capstone imprint. All rights reserved. No part of this publication may be reproduced in whole or in part, or stored in a retrieval system, or transmitted in any form or by any means, electronic, mechanical, photocopying, recording, or otherwise, without written permission of the publisher. For information regarding permission, write to Capstone Press, 1710 Roe Crest Drive, North Mankato, Minnesota 56003.

Library of Congress Cataloging-in-Publication Data
Cataloging-in-Publication Data is on file with the Library of Congress.
ISBN 978-1-4914-8489-0 (library binding)
ISBN 978-1-4914-8493-7 (paperback)
ISBN 978-1-4914-8497-5 (eBook PDF)

Editorial Credits
Brenda Haugen, editor; Sarah Bennett, designer; Wanda Winch, media researcher;
Katy LaVigne, production specialist

Photo Credits
Corbis, 11 (bottom), 17 (bottom), 23 (top), Don Troiani, 19, Leemage, 9, Royalty-Free, cover (bottom); CriaImages, 12, 22-23 (bottom), 26; Getty Images: Fotosearch, 13; Library of Congress: Prints and Photographs Division, 1 (bottom), 4, 11 (top), 15, 25, 29, Rare Book and Special Collections Division/ The Alfred Whital Stern Collection of Lincolniana, cover (top) 1 (top), 7, 18, 21, 27

Printed and bound in China. PO5070

TABLE OF CONTENTS

A NOTE ABOUT PRIMARY SOURCES

Primary sources are newspaper articles, photographs, speeches, or other documents that were created during an event. They are great ways to see how people spoke and felt during that time. You'll find primary sources from the time of the Civil War throughout this book. Within the text, primary source quotations are colored *brown* and set in italic type.

A DIVIDED NATION

Cannon fire boomed throughout and all around Fort Sumter on April 12, 1861. *"The roaring and crackling of the flames, the dense masses of whirling smoke, the bursting of the enemy's shells, and our own which were exploding in the burning rooms, the crashing of the shot, and the sound of masonry falling in every direction, made the fort a pandemonium,"* wrote Abner Doubleday, one of the fort's defenders.

▽ Confederate forces fired on Fort Sumter.

The **Union** fort sat on an island in the harbor of Charleston, South Carolina. South Carolina was one of the states in the newly formed **Confederacy**. The attack on Fort Sumter marked the opening battle of the Civil War (1861–1865), a war that had been brewing for decades. Northern states and southern states disagreed on many issues. The most important issue was slavery. Attempts to resolve the tensions had failed.

The war split the nation in two. It also split families. Fathers and sons often fought on opposite sides. So did brothers. Even husbands and wives were sometimes split in their loyalties.

The United States had struggled with the issue of slavery since the country had formed. Plantation owners in the South used slave labor to harvest cotton and other crops. So did the owners of some smaller southern farms. The cotton industry grew rapidly in the 19th century. To meet the growing demand, the number and size of plantations increased as well. Slavery became an even bigger part of the southern **economy**.

Union—the United States of America; also, the northern states that fought against the southern states in the Civil War
Confederacy—the southern states that fought against the northern states in the Civil War; also called the Confederate States of America
economy—system by which an area produces, distributes, and uses its money, goods, natural resources, and services

In the decades since the American Revolution, northern states had made it illegal to buy and sell slaves within their borders. Many northerners believed slavery should be abolished throughout the country, not just in the North. Only about one in four southern families owned slaves. Not all southerners supported slavery. Still, most southerners believed in the right to own slaves.

A series of compromises over several decades postponed war between the North and South. These included the Missouri Compromise of 1820, the Compromise of 1850, and the Kansas-Nebraska Act of 1854. Some of these actions tried to balance the number of free and slave states as new states formed. Others were designed to let voters in newly settled areas decide for themselves whether slavery would be allowed.

Henry Clay of Kentucky helped form the compromises of 1820 and 1850. Although he owned slaves, he disapproved of slavery as a practice. He wanted to set up a system that would release slaves gradually. Clay called slavery *"a violation of the rights of man."*

But the compromises only delayed addressing the key question. Would slavery be allowed to continue? Many people worried that slavery might split the nation apart.

Tensions boiled over after the election of President Abraham Lincoln in 1860. Lincoln pledged to keep slavery out of territories that were not yet states. Southerners feared he might try to end slavery everywhere. Lincoln tried to ease their fears. During his **Inaugural Address** on March 4, 1861, he said: *"I have no purpose, directly or indirectly, to interfere with the institution of slavery in the States where it exists."*

Lincoln's speech didn't help. By then seven states already had **seceded**. Four more soon followed. Jefferson Davis was named president of the Confederacy. In his Inaugural Address in February 1861, Davis said the Confederacy had *"merely asserted the right which the Declaration of Independence of 1776 defined to be inalienable."* The North and South were soon at war.

Inaugural Address—the speech a president gives when he or she is sworn into office
secede—to withdraw from
inalienable—impossible to take

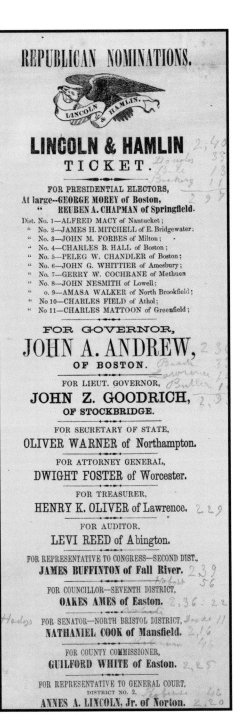

△ the Republican choices for office, showing Lincoln as their candidate for president of the United States

HOPES FOR A QUICK WAR FADE

Both the Union and Confederacy issued a call for troops. Thousands of young men volunteered. One Union recruiting poster offered a $150 cash payment to volunteers. That is more than $4,000 in today's dollars. The poster invited recruits to serve under *"the Flag of Our Union Forever and Ever!"* A Confederate poster said: *"Your soil has been invaded."* It called upon volunteers *"to rally at once, and drive them back."*

At first volunteers on both sides were eager to fight. Many feared the war would end before they could see action. Both sides thought that winning one or two battles would end the war quickly in their favor.

The Union army marched from Washington, D.C., in July 1861. It planned to attack southern troops gathered at Manassas, Virginia, about 30 miles (48 kilometers) away. Many onlookers traveled from Washington to watch the battle. They thought it would be fun to watch the Union soldiers gain a quick victory. Instead, Confederate troops turned back the Union attack after a fierce battle. Union soldiers and civilians fled back to Washington.

△ a Union army recruiting station in New York City in 1864

Nearly 200,000 African-Americans served as soldiers or sailors in the Union army and navy. The 54th Massachusetts Infantry Regiment was made up of black soldiers, led by a white commanding officer. They launched a famous attack on Fort Wagner, South Carolina, in July 1863. The attack failed, and many of the soldiers died. But observers praised their bravery. *"The Fifty-fourth did well and nobly,"* wrote war reporter Edward L. Pierce. The 1989 movie *Glory* honored the 54th.

Corporal Samuel English of Rhode Island described the retreat as being like a stampede. *"Off they started like a flock of sheep every man for himself,"* English wrote in a letter. This battle and several others in 1861 showed the war probably would not end quickly.

The reality of war soon sank in. As it did, the initial flood of volunteers slowed to a trickle. Both sides started to **draft** soldiers to fill their armies' ranks. Many people on both sides opposed the way the draft worked. Rich men could buy exemptions that allowed them to avoid serving in the army. Draft riots broke out in New York City. More than 100 people died, and hundreds more were injured.

△ Union troops marched out of Washington, D.C., to fight Confederate forces in Virginia.

▷ Guards attacked angry citizens during the New York draft riots.

CRITICAL THINKING

Why do you think the number of army volunteers on both sides dropped so much after the first few months of the war?

draft—to choose people who are compelled by law

BACK AND FORTH

The Union had many advantages during the war. It had a larger population from which to get soldiers. It had more factories to build weapons and supply troops. The Union also had a much larger navy. Until the war began, the Confederacy had no navy. The Union used its ships to **blockade** southern ports, harbors where ships docked. The South relied on supplies arriving from Europe. The blockade cut off much of that flow.

The Union also hoped to gain control of the Mississippi River. That river served as a way for the South to transport goods and troops. Union General Winfield Scott wrote that controlling the Mississippi River and blockading southern ports would *"bring them to terms with less bloodshed than by any other plan."*

Southern women stage a bread riot.

the North Atlantic Blockading Squadron in 1861

blockade—a military effort to keep goods from entering and

The blockade took a toll. Prices for bread, meat, and other foods skyrocketed in the South. Clothing was in short supply. More than 1,000 people staged a bread riot in Richmond, Virginia, in April 1863. Eyewitness John Jones asked where the angry crowd was going. In his diary, he wrote that one hungry-looking young woman responded that *"they were going to get something to eat."*

But the South had some advantages too. It fought most of the battles on its own soil. Soldiers and generals knew the best places to launch an attack or form a defensive line. They also knew the best places to cross rivers and streams. And while both sides had many experienced generals, several of the most brilliant and daring sided with the South.

The North focused much of its attention in 1862 on capturing Richmond. The Confederate capital was just over 100 miles (161 km) south of Washington, D.C. Despite having many more troops, the Union army was unable to achieve its goal. Sometimes, such as in the Seven Days Battles, southern General Robert E. Lee launched daring attacks against the larger Union army. He often used clever troop movements and the factor of surprise to help offset the Union army's greater number of troops. Lee's commanders, such as General Thomas Jonathan "Stonewall" Jackson and cavalry leader J.E.B. Stuart, helped carry out his plans. During one victory Lee remarked, *"It is well that war is so terrible—we should grow too fond of it."*

▷ Union and Confederate generals and statesmen as they appeared during the Civil War.

Both sides used spies to try to learn secrets about the enemy. One master of disguise was Franklin Thompson. Thompson was really Sarah Emma Edmonds. In a book based on her experiences, Edmonds described how she served as a Union soldier, nurse, and spy while disguised as a man. She wrote that she even once posed as a black man to sneak behind Confederate lines to learn about their troop strength. *"Perhaps a spirit of adventure was important,"* Edmonds later wrote, *"but patriotism was the grand secret of my success."*

Matters went better for the Union in the West. Union General Ulysses S. Grant won two key battles in early 1862. His army captured Confederate strongholds at Fort Henry and Fort Donelson. These forts guarded river access to key points in Tennessee and farther south. The Confederate commander at Fort Donelson proposed a meeting to discuss surrender terms. Grant replied, *"No terms except an unconditional and immediate surrender can be accepted."* After that, people joked that Grant's first two initials, U.S., stood for "unconditional surrender." The nickname stuck with Grant the rest of his life.

In addition, the Union captured the key port city of New Orleans, Louisiana, in April 1862. The South launched some attacks too, but major battles at Shiloh, Tennessee, and Perryville, Kentucky, forced them back.

The North got more good news in September. Lee's advance into the border state of Maryland stalled at the Battle of Antietam. The battle marked the war's single bloodiest day. More than 23,000 soldiers were killed, wounded, or missing. *"It was never my fortune to witness a more bloody, dismal battlefield,"* wrote Union General Joseph Hooker. The battle was a success for the North. Lee's attempt to invade the North had failed. His army retreated into Virginia.

Lincoln wanted to build on the success of Antietam. He soon released a document that put the purpose of the war in a whole new light.

▷ The Battle of Antietam was a great victory for the Union forces.

More than 600,000 soldiers died during the Civil War. Over half of them died of disease. About 30,000 wounded Union soldiers had limbs removed. Thousands of Confederates lost limbs too. These operations kept the death toll among the wounded soldiers from being even higher. William Blackford of Virginia said doctors *"armed with long, bloody knives and saws, cut and sawed away with frightful rapidity."*

17

As the war dragged on, more northerners were willing to let the South break away. Lincoln's Emancipation Proclamation, formally issued on January 1, 1863, helped combat that feeling. The proclamation said that all slaves in the rebellious areas *"are, and henceforward shall be free."*

But there was no way to enforce the proclamation. The slaveholding states in the Confederacy just ignored it. Still, the proclamation rallied support in the North. It confirmed that the war was about more than simply preserving the Union. It was a war mainly against slavery. It was a war for freedom. The proclamation also helped sway the opinions of foreign countries. Southerners had hoped that Great Britain and France would support their cause. Partly because of the Emancipation Proclamation, both nations stayed neutral. They opposed slavery.

GENERAL ORDERS, } No. 1. {

WAR DEPARTMENT, ADJUTANT GENERAL'S OFFICE, *Washington, January 2, 1863.*

The following Proclamation by the President is published for the information and government of the Army and all concerned:

BY THE PRESIDENT OF THE UNITED STATES OF AMERICA.

A PROCLAMATION.

WHEREAS, on the twenty-second day of September, in the year of our Lord one thousand eight hundred and sixty-two, a Proclamation was issued by the President of the United States, containing, among other things, the following, to wit:

"That on the first day of January, in the year of our Lord one thousand eight hundred and sixty-three, all persons held as slaves within any State or designated part of a State, the people whereof shall then be in rebellion against the United States, shall be then, thenceforward, and forever, free; and the Executive government of the United States, including the military and naval authority thereof, will recognize and maintain the freedom of such persons, and will do no act or acts to repress such persons, or any of them, in any efforts they may make for their actual freedom.

"That the Executive will, on the first day of January aforesaid, by proclamation, designate the States and parts of States, if any, in which the people thereof, respectively, shall then be in rebellion against the United States; and the fact that any State, or the people thereof, shall on that day be in good faith represented in the Congress of the United States, by members chosen thereto at elections wherein a majority of the qualified voters of such States shall have participated, shall, in the absence of strong countervailing testimony, be deemed conclusive evidence that such State, and the people thereof, are not then in rebellion against the United States."

Now, therefore, I, ABRAHAM LINCOLN, President of the United States, by virtue of the power in me vested as Commander-in-chief of

Δ publication of the Emancipation Proclamation by the U.S. War Department

△ The Battle of Gettysburg was a turning point in the war.

July 1863 brought two major northern victories. In early summer General Lee invaded Pennsylvania. He met General George Meade's army in a fierce and bloody three-day battle at Gettysburg. Each day the Confederates attacked the Union lines. Each day they failed to dislodge the Union troops. On the second day, fighting raged on a hill called Little Round Top. If the Confederates captured it, the whole Union defense might fall apart. Colonel Joshua Chamberlain led a small band of Maine soldiers in defending the hill. Chamberlain described the fighting as *"a struggle fierce and bloody beyond any that I have witnessed."* With ammunition running out, Chamberlain's troops launched a **bayonet** attack. Just when it appeared the Confederates might capture the hill, the daring Union charge forced them to retreat.

bayonet—a long metal blade attached to the end of a musket or rifle

On the third day, Lee ordered a charge on the center of the Union line. After suffering heavy losses, about 200 southern troops broke through. Union reinforcements quickly arrived. The southern troops could advance no farther. Many were killed, wounded, or captured. The point where the southern troops reached is marked with a monument calling the spot the *"High Water Mark of the Rebellion."* The next day Lee's army retreated. Roughly one of every three of its troops was killed, wounded, or missing. The South would never again be able to launch a major offensive.

At the same time, Union General Ulysses Grant finished a successful **siege** of the Confederate stronghold at Vicksburg, Mississippi. Once Vicksburg fell on July 4, the Union controlled the Mississippi River. This split the South in two. *"The fate of the Confederacy was sealed when Vicksburg fell,"* Grant later wrote. By the end of 1863, the North had gained the advantage.

siege—a military blockade of a place, to make it surrender

Bloody Battles

The Civil War cost more lives than any other war in U.S. history. About 620,000 soldiers died during the Civil War. Many died in battle. About two out of three, however, died of disease. Here are some of the bloodiest battles. The numbers include the dead, wounded, missing, and captured.

Battle	Union Casualties	Confederate Casualties	Total
Gettysburg	23,000	28,000	51,000
Chickamauga	16,170	18,454	34,624
Spotsylvania	18,000	12,000	30,000
The Wilderness	18,400	11,400	29,800
Chancellorsville	14,000	10,000	24,000
Shiloh	13,047	10,699	23,746
Stones River	13,249	10,266	23,515
Antietam	12,400	10,317	22,717

Four score and seven years ago our fathers brought forth on this continent, a new nation, conceived in Liberty, and dedicated to the proposition that all men are created equal.

Now we are engaged in a great civil war, testing whether that nation, or any nation so conceived and so dedicated, can long endure. We are met on a great battle-field of that war. We have come to dedicate a portion of that field, as a final resting place for those who here gave their lives that that nation might live. It is altogether fitting and proper that we should do this.

But, in a larger sense, we can not dedicate—we can not consecrate—we can not hallow—this ground. The brave men, living and dead, who struggled here, have consecrated it, far above our poor power to add or detract. The world will little note, nor long remember what we say here, but it can never forget what they did here. It is for us the living, rather, to be dedicated here to the unfinished work which they who fought here have thus far so nobly advanced. It is rather for us to be here dedicated to the great task remaining before us—that from these honored dead we take increased devotion to that cause for which they gave the last full measure of devotion—that we here highly resolve that these dead shall not have died in vain—that this nation, under God, shall have a new birth of freedom—and that government of the people, by the people, for the people, shall not perish from the earth.

Executive Mansion,
Washington

November 19. 1863.

Abraham Lincoln.

Four months after the Battle of Gettysburg, Lincoln spoke at an event to honor the fallen soldiers. His speech was short and simple. It began with the famous phrase: *"Four score and seven years ago…."* When Lincoln spoke that day, he didn't think his words had much impact. Over time his speech has come to be known as one of the greatest in history. In just a few words, he managed to sum up why the Civil War was so important.

◁ Abraham Lincoln's Gettysburg Address

CRITICAL THINKING

How might the outcome of the war have changed if the Confederates had won the Battle of Gettysburg?

GROWING PRESSURE

President Lincoln appointed Grant as commander of all the Union armies in 1864. Grant made good use of his larger troop numbers. The Union army kept attacking Lee's smaller force. Lee had no time to rest his troops or rebuild the army's supplies. The Union army drew closer and closer to Richmond.

Farther south, Union Admiral David Farragut won an important naval battle at the bay outside Mobile, Alabama, in August 1864. Mobile had been the last open port in the Gulf of Mexico east of Texas. At Mobile the Union ships faced mines, which at the time were called torpedoes. Farragut showed no fear. According to his aides, Farragut shouted, *"Damn the torpedoes! Full speed ahead."*

The Civil War marked the first battle between ironclad ships. Until then ships had been made of wood. The Confederate ironclad *Virginia* clashed with the Union ironclad *Monitor* in March 1862. The fierce battle ended with neither ship winning.

Union soldiers destroyed train tracks during General Sherman's "March to the Sea."

Union General William Tecumseh Sherman captured Atlanta, Georgia, in September 1864. Union troops burned down much of the city. Atlanta had been a major railroad center. Its loss cut southern supply lines. From there Sherman's soldiers marched through Georgia to the sea. They destroyed railroad tracks and took farmers' food and livestock as they went. Their goal was to convince the South that surrender was the only option. *"I can … make Georgia howl,"* Sherman said in a message to Grant.

the Battle of Mobile Bay

Despite these victories many people in the North continued to oppose the war. The Democratic Party nominated George McClellan to run against the Republican Lincoln in the 1864 presidential election. Early in the war McClellan had commanded the Union army. The Democratic Party's list of goals demanded *"immediate efforts be made for a cessation of hostilities."*

But all of the good news from the battlefield convinced voters that victory was near. They believed that soon the southern states would be forced back into the Union. Lincoln ended up easily winning reelection.

CRITICAL THINKING

Do you think the outcome of the Civil War might have been different if Abraham Lincoln had not won reelection? Why or why not?

▷ Candidates for president and vice president were featured in information about the 1864 election.

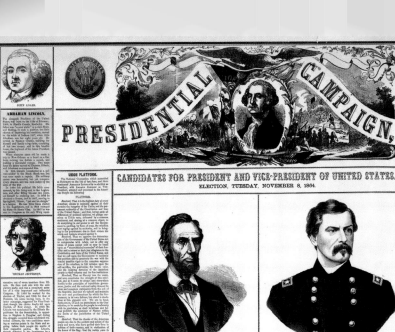

PRESIDENTIAL CAMPAIGN, 1864

CANDIDATES FOR PRESIDENT AND VICE-PRESIDENT OF UNITED STATES.

ELECTION, TUESDAY, NOVEMBER 8, 1864.

ABRAHAM LINCOLN, OF ILLINOIS.

GEORGE B. McCLELLAN, OF NEW JERSEY.

ANDREW JOHNSON, OF TENNESSEE.

GEORGE H. PENDLETON, OF OHIO.

MAP showing Loyal States in GREEN, what the Rebels still hold in RED, and what the Union Soldiers have wrested from them in YELLOW.

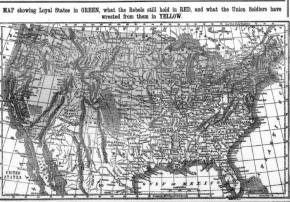

UNITED STATES.

ABRAHAM LINCOLN.

THOMAS JEFFERSON.

JAMES MADISON.

ANDREW JOHNSON.

JAMES MONROE.

JOHN TYLER.

ANDREW JACKSON.

MARTIN VAN BUREN.

W. H. HARRISON.

GEORGE H. PENDLETON.

JAMES BUCHANAN.

JOHN ADAMS.

GEO. BRINTON McCLELLAN.

JOHN QUINCY ADAMS.

DEMOCRATIC PLATFORM.

UNION PLATFORM.

McClellan's Letter of Acceptance.

Lincoln's Letter of Acceptance.

Popular Vote for President.

SINEWS OF THE REBELLION.

ELECTORAL COLLEGE.

Result of Presidential Elections in U.S. from 1796 to '60.

NATIONAL UNION EXECUTIVE COMMITTEE.

NATIONAL DEMOCRATIC EXECUTIVE COMMITTEE.

JAMES K. POLK.

ZACHARY TAYLOR.

MILLARD FILLMORE.

FRANKLIN PIERCE.

Published by H. H. LLOYD & CO., 21 John Street, New York.   B. B. RUSSELL, 515 Washington Street, Boston.   R. R. LANDON, 88 Lake Street, Chicago.

THE END AND A NEW BEGINNING

More than four years of fighting wound down in 1865. In March, at his second Inaugural Address, Lincoln knew victory was near. He called for peace *"with malice toward none; with charity for all."* In early April the Union army took control of Richmond. A week later Lee surrendered to Grant at Appomattox Court House, Virginia. As the news spread, other southern forces laid down their weapons as well.

▽ Generals Ulysses S. Grant (left) and Robert E. Lee signed the Confederate surrender at Appomattox Court House, Virginia.

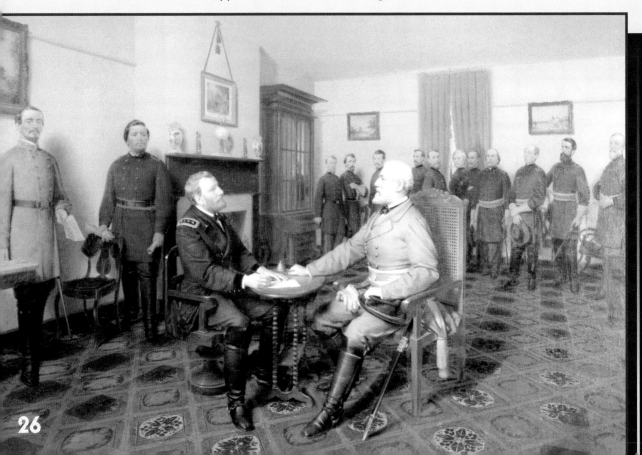

Lincoln wanted to bring the North and South back together as painlessly as possible. He never got a chance to see the process unfold. He was shot while attending a play on April 14 and died the next day. Lincoln's killer, John Wilkes Booth, shouted, *"Sic semper tyrannis!"* It means, "Thus ever to tyrants!"

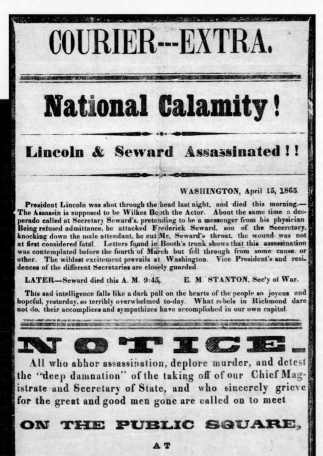

▽ A newspaper shared the news of President Lincoln's death.

COURIER---EXTRA.

National Calamity !

Lincoln & Seward Assassinated ! !

WASHINGTON, April 15, 1865.

President Lincoln was shot through the head last night, and died this morning.— The Assassin is supposed to be Wilkes Booth the Actor. About the same time a desperado called at Secretary Seward's, pretending to be a messenger from his physician Being refused admittance, he attacked Frederick Seward, son of the Secertary, knocking down the male attendant, he cut Mr. Seward's throat, the wound was not at first considered fatal. Letters found in Booth's trunk shows that this assassination was contemplated before the fourth of March but fell through from some cause, or other. The wildest excitement prevails at Washington. Vice President's and residences of the different Secretaries are closely guarded.

LATER—Seward died this A. M. 9:45.   E. M. STANTON, Sec'y of War.

This sad intelligence falls like a dark pall on the hearts of the people so joyous and hopeful, yesterday, so terribly overwhelmed to-day. What rebels in Richmond dare not do, their accomplices and sympathizes have accomplished in our own capitol.

NOTICE.

All who abhor assassination, deplore murder, and detest the "deep damnation" of the taking off of our Chief Magistrate and Secretary of State, and who sincerely grieve for the great and good men gone are called on to meet

ON THE PUBLIC SQUARE,

AT

3 O'clock, this afternoon, April 15, 1865.

Newspapers across the country spread the tragic news. *"Assassination of President Lincoln,"* reported the *New York Herald. "The President Shot at the Theatre Last Evening."* Even southern papers spoke out against the killing. The *Richmond Whig* said, *"the time, manner and circumstances of President Lincoln's death render it the most momentous, most appalling, most deplorable calamity which has ever befallen the people of the United States."*

The Civil War's end rejoined the nation, but it took the country decades to fully recover. Hundreds of thousands of young men on both sides had died. Areas of the South where fighting had taken place suffered heavy damage. Many farms and industries were destroyed. Atlanta had to be rebuilt. Southerners adjusted to a new economy that did not include slavery.

CRITICAL THINKING

How might the recovery process after the Civil War have been different if President Lincoln had not been killed?

A Huge Toll

The human cost of the Civil War was beyond anybody's expectations. The United States experienced bloodshed to a degree that has not been equaled in any other American conflict. The number of people who died during the Civil War was not equaled by the combined toll of all other American conflicts until the Vietnam War.

Civil War Deaths = 620,000

■ Revolutionary War = 25,000
■ War of 1812 = 15,000
■ Mexican War = 13,283
■ Spanish-American War = 2,446
■ World War I = 116, 516
■ World War II = 405,399
■ Korea = 36,516

■ Vietnam = 58,209
■ Gulf War = 294
■ Iraq-Afghanistan = 6,626

△ Some newly freed slaves gathered at Freedman's Village in Arlington, Virginia.

CRITICAL THINKING

If the South had won the Civil War, do you think the United States would ever have been reunited? Why or why not?

discrimination—treating a person or group unfairly, often because of their race or religion

The newly freed slaves faced many challenges too. They dealt with **discrimination** every day. In many cases they faced violence from southerners who did not want to accept their freedom. It took more than 100 years and many struggles for African-Americans to gain anything near their full rights as citizens.

The Civil War marked the biggest single challenge to the United States. The war's end allowed the nation to move forward. The country could again focus on forming new states in western areas. United again, the nation also moved toward becoming a major world power.

SELECTED BIBLIOGRAPHY

Civil War Trust. www.civilwar.org

"Conditions of Antibellum Slavery." PBS. www.pbs.org/wgbh/aia/

"Confederate States of America—Inaugural Address of the President of the Provisional Government." Avalon Project at Yale Law School. http://avalon.law.yale.edu/19th_century/

"Death and the Civil War." American Experience. www.pbs.org/wgbh/americanexperience/films/death/

"Economics and the Civil War." History Central.com. www.historycentral.com/CivilWar/AMERICA/Economics.html

Gettysburg National Military Park. National Park Service. www.nps.gov/gett/photosmultimedia/index.htm

Gienapp, William E. *Abraham Lincoln and Civil War America: A Biography.* Oxford, U.K.: Oxford University Press, 2002.

"Lincoln's First Inaugural Address." Digital History. www.digitalhistory.uh.edu/disp_textbook.cfm?smtID=3&psid=3873

McPherson, James M. *The Illustrated Battle Cry of Freedom: The Civil War Era.* New York: Oxford University Press, 2003.

Potter, David M. *The Impending Crisis, 1848—1861.* New York: Harper & Row, 1976.

Weigley, Russell F. *A Great Civil War: A Military and Political History, 1861—1865.* Bloomington, Ind.: Indiana University Press, 2000.

GLOSSARY

bayonet (BAY-uh-net)—a long metal blade attached to the end of a musket or rifle

blockade (blok-AYD)—a military effort to keep goods from entering and leaving a region

Confederacy (kuhn-FE-druh-see)—the southern states that fought against the northern states in the Civil War; also called the Confederate States of America

discrimination (dis-kri-muh-NAY-shuhn)—treating a person or group unfairly, often because of their race or religion

draft (DRAFT)—to choose people who are compelled by law to serve in the military

economy (i-KAH-nuh-mee)—system by which an area produces, distributes, and uses its money, goods, natural resources, and services

inalienable (in-AYL-yuh-nuh-buhl)—impossible to take away or give up

Inaugural Address (in-AW-gyer-uhl uh-DRESS)—the speech a president gives when he or she is sworn into office

secede (si-SEED)—to withdraw from

siege (SEEJ)—a military blockade of a place, to make it surrender

Union (YOON-yuhn)—the United States of America; also, the northern states that fought against the southern states in the Civil War

INTERNET SITES

FactHound offers a safe, fun way to find Internet sites related to this book. All of the sites on FactHound have been researched by our staff.

Here's all you do:

Visit *www.facthound.com*

Type in this code: 9781491484890

 Check out projects, games and lots more at
www.capstonekids.com

INDEX